AF413507

PIONEERING SPIRIT

WOMEN'S PURSUITS IN OVERCOMING BARRIERS AND ACHIEVING POWER

DR. MINAKSHI BANSAL

DEDICATION

Dedicated to the trailblazers and the quiet revolutionaries, to the women who have paved the way with their resilience and to those who continue to light the path forward with their courage. This book honors all women who lead, challenge, and change the world every day without fail. May their strength inspire generations to come.

ϷϷϷ

Contents

Contents

Prayer

"Om Bhadram Karnebhih Shrinuyama Devah
Bhadram Pashyemakshabhiryajatrah
Sthirairangais Tushtuvamsastanubhih
Vyashema Devahitam Yadayuh
Svasti Na Indro Vriddhashravah
Svasti Nah Pusha Vishwavedah
Svasti Nastarkshyo Arishtanemih
Svasti No Brihaspatir Dadhatu
Om Shantih Shantih Shantih"

This mantra is a prayer for universal well-being, invoking the blessings of various deities for protection, health, and happiness. It emphasizes the importance of experiencing the auspicious through all senses and living a life aligned with divine purpose. The repetition of "Shantih" at the end signifies a deep desire for peace in the individual, the environment, and the universe at large. This mantra is often recited as a prayer for peace, prosperity, and the physical and spiritual well-being of all beings.

ϼϼϼ

About The Author

Dr. Minakshi Bansal, born in the bustling metropolis of Delhi, India, has led a life steeped in artistry, scholarly pursuit, and an unwavering commitment to societal betterment. Following her marriage, she relocated to Ahmedabad, Gujarat, where she has since blossomed into a multifaceted beacon of inspiration for many. Dr. Minakshi is not only recognized as a gifted artist in the realm of Fine Arts but also as an esteemed author, a devoted social worker and a dedicated research scholar in Psychology. Her journey, marked by a profound dedication to elevating those around her, especially the downtrodden and underprivileged children of society, is a testament to her deep-seated belief in the transformative power of engagement and empathy.

From her earliest days, Minakshi was distinguished by an insatiable appetite for reading. Her literary universe was inhabited by characters and narratives that spanned ethical tales, motivational and inspirational stories, and the mythic parables imbued with life lessons. This voracious reading habit was not merely for personal edification but was driven by a desire to distill and disseminate the essence of these narratives to foster the development of students and peers alike. She was particularly captivated by the lives and teachings of historical figures and spiritual leaders such as Adi Shankaracharya, Swami Vivekananda, Dr. APJ Abdul Kalam, Mahamana Pandit Madan Mohan Malviya, Mahatma Gandhi, Sardar Vallabhai Patel, and Vinoba Bhave, among others. Their philosophies and life stories fueled her ambition to embody their ideals of resilience, selflessness, and relentless pursuit of knowledge.

Dr. Minakshi's academic and practical engagement with psychology has been equally noteworthy. As a research scholar, her focus has been on exploring the intricate tapestry of the human psyche, aiming to unlock the potential for psychological well-being and societal harmony. Her scholarly work is complemented by her active involvement in social work, where she employs her academic insights to make tangible differences in the lives of the underprivileged. Her endeavours in social work are characterized by an innovative approach that combines traditional wisdom with contemporary psychological practices to address the multifaceted challenges faced by these communities.

Her artistic talents, another facet of her diverse capabilities, are not merely a personal passion but also serve as a medium through which she communicates and connects with others. Her art, rich in symbolism and emotional depth, reflects her philosophical inquiries and social concerns, offering viewers a glimpse into the breadth of her intellect and the depth of her compassion.

In addition to her contributions to the arts and social sciences, Dr. Minakshi has embraced the healing arts of Pranic Healing, mastering the techniques developed by Master Choa Kok Sui. This practice, which focuses on the manipulation of Prana or life energy to heal the body and aura, has been both a personal journey of discovery and a means through which she extends her healing touch to others. Her proficiency in Pranic Healing is complemented by her advocacy and teaching of various forms of meditation aimed at rejuvenation, personal betterment, and the cultivation of harmony within individuals and communities alike.

Dr. Minakshi's life is a narrative of relentless pursuit, not just of personal achievement but of the upliftment and empowerment of society at large. Her diverse interests and talents—spanning the arts, literature, psychology, and the healing practices—converge on a singular path of service. She embodies the spirit of the luminaries who inspired her, channelling their legacy through her actions and teachings. Through her books, art, and social initiatives, she continues to inspire a new generation to embark on their own journeys of self-discovery, resilience, and altruism.

Her commitment to social betterment, particularly her focus on uplifting underprivileged children, reflects a deep understanding of the transformative potential of education and personal development. By integrating her knowledge of psychology, her artistic sensibilities, and her healing practices, Dr. Bansal has developed a holistic approach to social work that addresses both the immediate needs and the long-term well-being of the communities she serves.

As an author, Dr. Minakshi's writings offer a blend of inspirational insights, practical wisdom, and reflective contemplations drawn from her extensive reading and life experiences. Her books serve as a guide for those seeking to navigate the complexities of life with grace, resilience, and purpose. Through her narratives, she extends an invitation to her readers to explore the depths of their own potential and to contribute meaningfully to the collective well-being of society.

In Dr. Minakshi Bansal, we find a remarkable synthesis of the artist, the scholar, the healer, and the social activist. Her life's work stands as a beacon of hope and a source of inspiration for individuals seeking to make a difference in the world. Her story is a compelling reminder of the power of individual action, rooted in compassion and driven by a profound commitment to the betterment of humanity. Dr. Minakshi's legacy is not just in the tangible outcomes of her efforts but in the enduring spirit of inquiry, empathy, and service that she embodies.

ppp

Preface

In the journey to leadership, women often traverse a path paved with unique challenges and remarkable triumphs. This book is borne out of a deep desire to explore these very pathways, highlighting not just the barriers women face as they climb to positions of power, but also celebrating the grace with which they overcome these obstacles. As we delve into the lives and careers of various women leaders, we discover a rich tapestry of stories that are both inspiring and instructive.

The pursuit of leadership is rarely straightforward and is often more complicated for women due to a myriad of social, cultural, and organizational hurdles. These barriers can be as overt as institutional sexism or as subtle as the biases that influence daily interactions and decisions. Yet, despite these challenges, women across the globe continue to make significant strides, breaking ceilings of glass and expectations alike. This narrative is not just about leadership; it's about leadership achieved against the odds, leadership carved out in spaces that were not designed to accommodate it.

What does it mean to lead with grace? This question lies at the heart of our exploration. Grace is often mistaken for mere politeness, a superficial gentility that connotes weakness. However, the grace of which we speak in this context is a powerful amalgamation of resilience, courage, and the unyielding strength to stay the course. It is the poised determination that enables women to navigate the complexities of leadership with foresight and fortitude.

The stories included in this analysis span continents and industries, reflecting a diverse range of experiences and insights. From the boardrooms of Fortune 500 companies to the front lines of nonprofit organizations, women leaders are not only contributing to economic growth but are also driving social change. Their leadership styles, often collaborative and inclusive, bring new dimensions to strategies and solutions in the modern workplace.

Moreover, the influence of technology and globalization on women's leadership cannot be understated. These forces have opened up new platforms for visibility and exchange, allowing women to build networks of influence that transcend geographical boundaries. Social media, in particular, has become a powerful tool for women to express their voices, share their experiences, and advocate for change. It also presents new challenges and arenas where gender dynamics play out in complex ways.

Education and empowerment emerge as recurrent themes in these narratives. The transformative power of education in shaping leaders is evident, as is the role of personal development and continuous learning in sustaining leadership. Mentorship, too, plays a crucial role in guiding and inspiring the next generation of women leaders, providing them with the wisdom and tools needed to navigate their own leadership journeys.

Another significant aspect of this discussion is the ethical dimension of leadership. Women often bring to their leadership roles an inherent focus on ethics and corporate social responsibility, championing not only growth but also sustainability and community engagement. This ethical approach often prompts a reassessment of organizational values and strategies, aligning them more closely with the ideals of equity, transparency, and long-term societal benefit.

As we look to the future, the landscape of women's leadership is poised for dramatic shifts. With increasing global attention on gender equality and an expanding body of research supporting the benefits of diverse leadership, the prospects for women in leadership are expanding. Yet, the path is not without its forthcoming challenges. The ongoing struggle for equality, the balancing of myriad roles, and the breaking of the final layers of glass ceilings will require not only individual resilience but also systemic change.

This book is crafted for anyone who seeks to understand the nuances of women's leadership and is especially relevant for young women aspiring to lead, for organizations aiming to harness the benefits of diverse leadership, and for policymakers dedicated to creating equitable frameworks in business and governance. It is a call to acknowledge, celebrate, and amplify the role of women in leadership across all spheres of life.

By chronicling these journeys, this book aims to inspire, educate, and provoke thought about the complex interplay of factors that influence women's leadership. It is a tribute to the indomitable spirit of women who lead, and a toolkit for those who aspire to join their ranks. Leadership, especially when pursued with grace and resilience, is a testament to the power of women to reshape the world. As we move forward, let us carry with us the lessons of these leaders, crafting a future where power is not merely held but is wielded to create a more just and equitable society.

Dr. Minakshi Bansal
Social Activist
Ahmedabad, Gujarat, Bharat

ppp

ONE

BREAKING THE GLASS CEILING: STORIES OF TRIUMPH

The metaphor of the glass ceiling captures the invisible yet seemingly impenetrable barrier that prevents women from rising to the upper rungs of the corporate ladder, regardless of their qualifications or achievements. This chapter delves into the experiences of various women who have faced and shattered these ceilings, offering insights into the strategies they employed and the resilience they exhibited.

The journey begins with the recognition of the glass ceiling's existence. Historically, corporate leadership has been dominated by men, creating an environment where women often struggle to be seen as equals. Despite the progress made in gender equality, women continue to be underrepresented in executive roles. However, numerous stories of triumph emerge from those who have managed to overcome these challenges.

One key strategy employed by successful women is the cultivation of a robust professional network. Networking allows women to connect with mentors and sponsors who can provide guidance, opportunities, and advocacy. These relationships are crucial, as they often give women a leg up in accessing roles that might otherwise be inaccessible. For example, a study by a leading business school found that women who actively engage in formal and informal networking events are more likely to be promoted than those who do not.

Mentorship is another vital component. Women leaders often cite the influence of a mentor who has guided them through the nuances of navigating a male-dominated business environment. These mentors not only offer advice and feedback but also help women build confidence in their leadership style and decision-making.

Resilience is perhaps the most critical attribute that these women exhibit. The path to the top is fraught with challenges, from overt discrimination to subtler forms of bias. Successful women leaders share stories of resilience, describing how they overcame setbacks and continued to pursue their goals with determination and grace. They often speak of the importance of learning from failure, not as a deterrent but as a stepping stone to greater success.

Innovation in leadership style also plays a significant role. Women often bring different perspectives and approaches to leadership, which can be particularly effective in driving organizational change. Their focus on collaborative and empathetic leadership can lead to higher team cohesion and improved problem-solving capabilities. This shift in leadership style not only helps in breaking personal glass ceilings but also promotes a more inclusive culture within the organization.

Finally, personal branding has emerged as a powerful tool for women aiming to break the glass ceiling. By developing a strong personal brand, women can establish themselves as experts in their fields, gain visibility, and influence their industries. This involves not only excelling at their jobs but also being active participants in industry conversations, speaking at conferences, and contributing to relevant publications.

Through these stories of triumph, it becomes evident that while the glass ceiling is a daunting barrier, it is not insurmountable. The combination of networking, mentorship, resilience, innovative leadership, and strong personal branding forms a formidable arsenal that women can use to claim their rightful places in leadership. As more women continue to break through these barriers, they not only achieve personal success but also pave the way for others to follow, ultimately enriching the leadership landscape with diversity and dynamism.

These narratives not only inspire but also provide a blueprint for how women in various stages of their careers can strategize their rise to the top. They serve as a testament to the power of perseverance and the importance of supporting one another, reinforcing the idea that the glass ceiling, however tough it may seem, can indeed be broken.

ppp

"*True leadership is marked not by dominance but by the ability to inspire and empower others—a quality many women naturally embody.*"

❧❧❧

TWO

MENTORSHIP AND ITS ROLE IN WOMEN'S LEADERSHIP

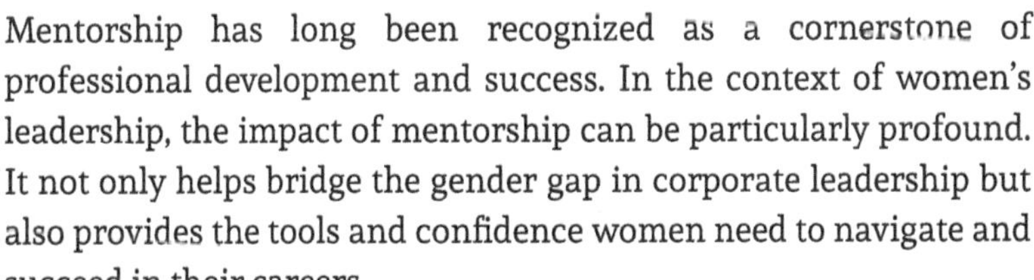

Mentorship has long been recognized as a cornerstone of professional development and success. In the context of women's leadership, the impact of mentorship can be particularly profound. It not only helps bridge the gender gap in corporate leadership but also provides the tools and confidence women need to navigate and succeed in their careers.

Mentorship for women often goes beyond mere career guidance. It encompasses the development of leadership skills, navigation of workplace dynamics, and the intricate balancing of professional and personal life. Women mentoring women has shown to foster an environment where female leaders can thrive, breaking down barriers and setting new standards in traditionally male-dominated arenas.

Building a Supportive Network

One of the primary benefits of mentorship is the establishment of a supportive network. Women often face unique challenges in the workplace, such as gender bias and fewer opportunities for advancement. A mentor who has navigated similar challenges can offer invaluable advice on overcoming these obstacles. Furthermore, mentors can introduce mentees to influential networks which are often inaccessible. These connections are vital for career progression and can often dictate the pace at which a woman ascends in her career path.

Developing Leadership Skills

Mentorship also plays a critical role in the development of essential leadership skills. Effective leadership requires a diverse array of skills, from strategic thinking to emotional intelligence. Women in leadership positions can mentor emerging female leaders by sharing their insights and experiences, which are often shaped by navigating a corporate landscape that may not have been originally designed to support them. This real-world knowledge is crucial for young women who aspire to lead, providing them with a roadmap to develop their own leadership style.

Overcoming Gender Bias

Gender bias remains a significant barrier in many professional fields. Women are often subjected to stereotypes that can impede their progress or influence the perception of their capabilities. Mentors help by preparing women to handle such biases effectively. They share strategies that have worked for them, such as how to assert authority in meetings or how to ensure their ideas are heard and respected. This mentorship aspect is vital in empowering women to push back against biases and advocate for themselves.

Career Strategy and Progression

Navigating career progression requires a strategic approach, especially for women who aspire to break into senior leadership roles. Mentors help in identifying opportunities for growth, advising on career moves, and providing feedback on performance. They can also offer guidance on educational advancements or skill development necessary for climbing the career ladder. This strategic guidance is crucial in a corporate world where career paths can often be less transparent or accessible for women.

Fostering Empathy and Emotional Intelligence

An often overlooked aspect of mentorship is the development of empathy and emotional intelligence. These qualities are increasingly recognized as hallmarks of effective leadership. Women leaders can mentor others not just through professional advice but also by demonstrating empathy. This can create more collaborative and innovative working environments, which are key to organizational success. Mentors who emphasize the importance of understanding and managing one's own emotions and those of others contribute significantly to the development of well-rounded leaders.

Personal Growth and Self-Confidence

Finally, mentorship contributes significantly to personal growth and self-confidence. For many women, having a mentor who believes in their potential can make a substantial difference in their self-perception and ambition. This boost in confidence is often reflected in their work performance and interactions with colleagues and superiors, enabling them to take on new challenges and assert their place in leadership roles confidently.

The role of mentorship in promoting women's leadership cannot be overstated. It provides not only professional guidance and network expansion but also personal growth and resilience-building. Through these relationships, women gain the confidence and skills necessary to navigate the complexities of the workplace and to ascend to leadership positions. As more women take on mentorship roles, they create a ripple effect, empowering a new generation of female leaders who are ready to challenge the status quo and lead with confidence and capability. These mentorship relationships are not just professional exchanges; they are transformative experiences that help shape the leaders of tomorrow.

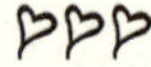

"The glass ceiling is not just a barrier to be shattered, but a reminder of the resilience and determination that women bring to the table every day."

❥❥❥

THREE

BALANCING THE SCALES: FAMILY AND CAREER

The quest to balance family and career is a central theme in the lives of many women. This delicate balancing act involves managing the demands of a successful career while fulfilling family responsibilities. The complexity of this balance can vary greatly from one individual to another, depending on career goals, family dynamics, and personal aspirations. Despite these challenges, many women successfully navigate these waters, providing valuable strategies and insights for others.

The Evolution of Work-Life Balance

Historically, the burden of balancing family and career has disproportionately fallen on women. Societal expectations often dictate that women should prioritize family over professional ambitions. However, as societal norms evolve, there is a growing recognition of the importance of both parents playing active roles in family and domestic responsibilities. This shift has facilitated a more equitable distribution of family duties, allowing women greater freedom to pursue their careers.

The evolution towards a more balanced division of labor in the home is paralleled by changes in the workplace. Increasingly, companies are implementing policies that promote work-life balance, recognizing that supportive work environments contribute to higher productivity and employee satisfaction. These policies might include flexible working hours, remote work options, and parental leave for both mothers and fathers.

Challenges Faced by Women

Despite these advancements, women often face significant challenges when trying to balance family and career. One of the major hurdles is the "motherhood penalty," a term used to describe the systematic disadvantages that mothers often encounter in the workplace, such as lower pay, reduced opportunities for advancement, and perceived lack of commitment to their job. Conversely, men often experience a "fatherhood bonus," where they are perceived as more stable and committed after becoming parents.

Another challenge is the mental load, a concept referring to the constant planning, organizing, remembering, and multitasking involved in managing a household and family, which disproportionately falls on women. This can lead to burnout and stress, as the mental load is often invisible and undervalued.

Strategies for Balancing Family and Career

To manage the dual demands of family and career, many women employ specific strategies. Prioritizing and setting clear boundaries is crucial. This might mean defining specific work hours and sticking to them, or learning to say no to requests that interfere with family time or personal well-being.

Time management is another vital skill. Effective use of time, whether through delegation of tasks at work or home, can help in maintaining a balance. Technology can aid in this area, with various apps and tools designed to streamline tasks and manage time more efficiently.

Flexibility in work arrangements can also make a significant difference. Telecommuting, flexible hours, and job-sharing are examples of how flexibility can be integrated into the workplace to help employees manage their family and work commitments better.

Support Systems and Networks

A robust support system is invaluable for balancing family and career. This support can come from a variety of sources: spouses, family members, friends, and professional networks. Sharing responsibilities at home, seeking emotional support, and leveraging professional connections can alleviate some of the pressures faced by working mothers.

In addition, many women find it beneficial to connect with others in similar situations. Support groups, whether formal or informal, provide a space to share experiences, offer advice, and gain emotional support. These networks can be particularly important in providing role models and mentors who have navigated similar challenges.

Personal Well-being and Self-care

Lastly, personal well-being and self-care are critical components of maintaining balance. The demands of juggling family and career can be physically and emotionally draining. It is essential for women to prioritize their health and well-being to sustain their ability to meet these demands. This can include regular exercise, healthy eating, sufficient sleep, and time for relaxation and hobbies.

Balancing family and career is an ongoing and dynamic challenge, requiring constant adjustment and negotiation. However, with supportive policies, effective strategies, and robust networks, women can manage these dual responsibilities successfully. The stories of countless women who navigate these challenges every day are not only testament to their resilience and strength but also serve as inspiration and guidance for others striving to achieve their own balance.

❦❦❦

"In navigating male-dominated fields, women do not merely strive to fit in; they reshape these spaces to embrace inclusivity and diversity."

ᗡᗡᗡ

FOUR

Navigating Male-Dominated Industries

Navigating male-dominated industries presents a unique set of challenges and opportunities for women. These industries, which include sectors like technology, engineering, construction, and finance, have traditionally been characterized by a significant gender imbalance, presenting barriers that can affect a woman's career trajectory and professional experience. Understanding these challenges and adopting effective strategies can significantly enhance the ability of women to succeed and lead in these environments.

Understanding the Landscape

The first step in navigating male-dominated industries is understanding the landscape. These sectors often have deeply ingrained cultural norms and practices that can perpetuate gender disparities. For example, women might find themselves being the only female in team meetings or being overlooked in discussions where male voices predominate. Recognizing these patterns is crucial to developing strategies to address them effectively.

Challenges in Male-Dominated Industries

Women in these industries often encounter several common challenges. One significant challenge is the lack of female role models. Without visible mentors or leaders who share similar gender experiences, it can be difficult for women to envision their path to success and leadership. This lack of representation can also affect the aspirations of younger women entering the industry.

Another major challenge is dealing with explicit or implicit bias. Women may face stereotypes about their capabilities, especially in technical or physical roles traditionally dominated by men. These biases can affect hiring decisions, performance evaluations, and opportunities for advancement.

Sexual harassment and inappropriate behavior are also more prevalent in male-dominated industries. Such environments can create hostile or unwelcoming work conditions, impacting women's job satisfaction and longevity in the field.

Strategies for Success

Despite these challenges, there are several effective strategies that women can employ to navigate and succeed in male-dominated industries.

Building Credibility

One critical strategy is building credibility. This can be achieved through demonstrating competence and confidence in one's role. Women can invest in continuous learning and skills development to ensure they are experts in their field. Being well-prepared and knowledgeable can help counteract stereotypes and earn respect from colleagues and supervisors.

Networking and Support

Developing a robust professional network is another key strategy. Networking within and outside of one's organization can provide support, advice, and opportunities. It is also beneficial to seek out or establish groups for women within the industry, which can offer a platform for sharing experiences and strategies for overcoming common challenges.

Effective Communication

Mastering effective communication skills is essential. This includes being assertive and clear in communication, ensuring that one's ideas and contributions are heard and recognized. It also involves learning to negotiate for promotions, raises, and leadership opportunities, which is crucial for career advancement.

Finding Allies and Advocates

Having allies in the workplace, both male and female, can significantly impact a woman's career in a male-dominated industry. Allies can help advocate for a woman's contributions and skills, include them in important meetings, and provide support in instances of bias or discrimination. These relationships are often built through mutual respect and professional collaboration.

Personal Resilience and Adaptation

Personal resilience is crucial when facing setbacks or biases. Women in male-dominated industries often need to develop a thick skin and an ability to adapt to challenging situations without compromising their integrity or professional standards. This includes handling criticism constructively and learning from every experience to improve continuously.

Creating Change

Lastly, women who achieve success in male-dominated industries often have the opportunity to create change for those who follow. By actively participating in mentorship, advocating for inclusive policies, and leading by example, they can help transform the industry culture, making it more welcoming and equitable for other women.

Navigating male-dominated industries requires a multifaceted approach, involving personal development, strategic networking, effective communication, and resilience. By employing these strategies, women can overcome barriers and establish themselves as leaders, paving the way for greater gender diversity and inclusion in their fields. These efforts not only benefit the individual women but also contribute to the broader cultural shift towards more inclusive and diverse industry practices.

ppp

"Mentorship for women, by women, creates an unbreakable chain of empowerment that transcends generations and industries."

❦❦❦

FIVE

Cultural Expectations and Women's Leadership

Cultural expectations play a profound role in shaping the landscape of women's leadership. These expectations can vary significantly across different societies, influencing how women perceive their own potential for leadership and how they are perceived by others. Understanding and navigating these cultural norms is crucial for women who aspire to lead, as well as for organizations aiming to foster more inclusive environments.

The Impact of Culture on Leadership

Culture deeply influences what is considered acceptable or desirable behavior in leaders. In many cultures, leadership traits are traditionally associated with masculinity, such as assertiveness, aggression, and independence. Women, often stereotypically associated with attributes like empathy, cooperation, and nurturing, may find themselves at odds with these traditional leadership models. This discrepancy can lead to women's leadership abilities being underestimated or undervalued, impacting their advancement opportunities.

Challenging Stereotypes

One of the primary challenges women face is the stereotype of what a leader should look like. These stereotypes are not only about gender but also about the intersectionality of race, ethnicity, and class. Women often need to navigate complex social dynamics that may question their authority or leadership style. Challenging these stereotypes requires not only individual resilience and adaptability but also a concerted effort from organizations to promote diversity in leadership models.

Dual Burden of Professional and Domestic Roles

Culturally, women are often expected to bear the primary responsibility for domestic roles, including childcare, eldercare, and household management. This dual burden can limit their availability and energy for professional growth, especially in demanding leadership roles. Addressing this issue often requires significant changes both in the workplace and at home, including more supportive policies from employers and a more equitable distribution of domestic responsibilities.

Strategies for Overcoming Cultural Barriers

Women can adopt several strategies to overcome the cultural barriers to leadership. These include:

Education and Awareness

Increasing awareness about the impact of cultural expectations on women's leadership is essential. Education plays a crucial role here, both in formal settings and through media and social platforms. Highlighting stories of successful women leaders and discussing the challenges they face can help change perceptions and inspire other women.

Building Support Networks

Creating and participating in support networks can provide women with the resources, mentorship, and encouragement needed to pursue leadership roles. These networks can be particularly valuable in cultures where women may not traditionally hold leadership positions. They provide a sense of solidarity and shared purpose, helping women navigate their professional journeys together.

Developing Leadership Skills

Women can actively seek opportunities to develop and demonstrate leadership skills. This might include pursuing leadership roles in volunteer organizations, attending leadership development programs, or seeking roles that stretch their capabilities within their workplaces. By building a robust portfolio of leadership experiences, women can challenge the cultural norms that might otherwise limit their opportunities.

Negotiating Work-Life Balance

Successfully negotiating work-life balance is crucial. This might involve advocating for policies that support work-life integration, such as flexible working hours, telecommuting options, and parental leave. It also involves setting personal boundaries to ensure that time for family and self-care are maintained.

Advocacy and Policy Change

Finally, advocating for policy changes that support women's leadership is crucial. This can include efforts to ensure equal pay, anti-discrimination practices, and policies that support women in leadership roles. Women in leadership positions can leverage their influence to advocate for these changes, not only within their organizations but also at a broader societal level.

Navigating Cultural Dynamics

Understanding and navigating the cultural dynamics that influence leadership can help women more effectively address the challenges they face. This involves recognizing the diverse cultural contexts in which women operate and developing strategies that are sensitive to these nuances. By doing so, women can not only advance their own careers but also contribute to a more diverse and inclusive leadership paradigm.

As more women break through cultural barriers and take on leadership roles, they pave the way for future generations to redefine leadership in culturally diverse contexts. This ongoing transformation is essential for creating more equitable and effective organizations and societies, where leadership is reflective of the diversity of its members.

▷▷▷

"Networking isn't just about building connections;
it's about weaving a fabric of mutual support and
opportunity that uplifts everyone."

ᐳᐳᐳ

SIX

THE POWER OF NETWORKING AND BUILDING ALLIANCES

Networking and building alliances are critical components of professional success, particularly for women who often face unique barriers in career advancement. Effective networking can open doors to new opportunities, provide essential support systems, and foster collaborations that might not otherwise be available. For women aiming to ascend to leadership positions or to thrive in their chosen fields, the ability to cultivate meaningful relationships and alliances is indispensable.

The Importance of Networking

Networking involves more than simply collecting business cards or adding connections on LinkedIn. It is about building relationships that are mutually beneficial, where support, information, and resources can be exchanged. For women, networking can be a powerful tool to combat the isolation that sometimes accompanies being one of the few women in a company or industry. It can also counteract the effects of exclusion from informal networks, such as those traditionally dominated by men.

Overcoming Barriers to Networking

Women may encounter specific challenges when trying to build their professional networks. These can include limited access to networking opportunities, the struggle to break into existing networks that may be male-dominated, or even subconscious biases that affect the willingness of others to engage professionally with women. Recognizing these barriers is the first step toward overcoming them.

Strategies for Effective Networking

Developing a robust network requires intentional efforts, and there are several strategies that women can use to enhance their networking effectiveness:

Attend Industry and Networking Events

Attending industry conferences, seminars, and networking events is a traditional and effective way to meet new people and establish professional connections. Women should aim to attend these events regularly and engage actively. This includes participating in discussions, asking questions, and following up on connections made during events.

Leverage Social Media Platforms

Social media platforms like LinkedIn, Twitter, and industry-specific forums provide powerful tools for networking. Women can use these platforms to connect with peers, join professional groups, share their achievements, and contribute to discussions. Social media also allows for the maintenance of relationships over distances that would otherwise be prohibitive.

Create and Participate in Peer Groups

Creating or joining peer support groups can provide a platform for sharing experiences, resources, and advice. These groups can be particularly beneficial for women in male-dominated industries, as they provide a space to discuss specific challenges and strategies for overcoming them.

Seek Mentors and Become a Mentor

Mentorship is a profound aspect of networking. Seeking out mentors can provide guidance, support, and advocacy. At the same time, becoming a mentor to others can strengthen one's network and establish one's reputation as a leader and expert in the field.

Build Alliances Across Genders

While women can benefit enormously from networks comprised of other women, it is also important to build alliances with men. In many fields, men still hold the majority of leadership positions, and having male allies can facilitate access to influential networks, provide different perspectives, and help advocate for gender diversity.

Networking with Purpose and Authenticity

Effective networking is not just about expanding one's professional circle; it should also be purposeful and authentic. This means building relationships based on genuine interests and mutual respect, rather than seeing connections merely as steps on a ladder to personal success. Authentic relationships are more likely to provide meaningful support and long-lasting professional engagement.

The Benefits of Strong Alliances

The alliances formed through networking can lead to numerous benefits. They can provide insights into upcoming opportunities, offer support during professional challenges, and enhance one's influence within an industry. Alliances can also lead to collaborations that combine diverse skills and perspectives, leading to innovative solutions and ventures.

Navigating and Enhancing Professional Relationships

Maintaining and nurturing professional relationships is as important as building them. Regular communication, sharing of resources, and mutual support are essential to ensure that networks remain vibrant and beneficial. Women who invest in their networks and alliances can see substantial returns in terms of career opportunities, professional development, and personal growth.

Networking and building alliances are indispensable tools for professional advancement, particularly for women navigating the complexities of modern career landscapes. By strategically building and maintaining diverse networks, women can enhance their career trajectories, contribute to their fields, and pave the way for more inclusive, supportive professional environments.

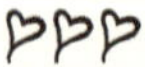

"Assertiveness in leadership involves clear communication, the courage to stand firm in one's convictions, and the wisdom to listen and adapt."

ᐅᐅᐅ

SEVEN

OVERCOMING BIAS: TACTICS AND STRATEGIES

Bias in the workplace is a significant barrier that many women face, affecting everything from hiring practices to daily interactions and long-term career progression. While bias can sometimes be overt, it often manifests in subtle, systemic ways that can be difficult to pinpoint and challenge. For women aiming to advance their careers and achieve leadership roles, developing strategies to overcome these biases is crucial.

Understanding the Types of Bias

Bias in the workplace can take many forms. Explicit biases are conscious beliefs or behaviors that openly discriminate against certain groups. In contrast, implicit biases are unconscious associations and attitudes that can influence decision-making and actions without explicit awareness. Women often encounter both types in their professional lives, including gender biases, racial biases, and biases related to age or parental status.

Strategies to Overcome Bias

Several effective strategies can help women address and overcome biases in the workplace:

Education and Awareness Training

One of the first steps in overcoming bias is to ensure that everyone in the organization is aware of its existence and understands its effects. Many companies now implement diversity training programs that help employees recognize and address their biases. While not a solution on their own, these programs can be a valuable part of a broader strategy to reduce bias.

Seeking Allyship and Building Support Networks

Allies can play a crucial role in helping to overcome workplace biases. Allies are individuals who support those different from themselves, advocating for inclusion and equity within the workplace. Women can benefit from seeking out allies across different levels of the organization, including peers, subordinates, and leaders who can influence change and provide support in challenging biased behaviors and policies.

Enhancing Visibility and Assertiveness

Women can combat bias by enhancing their visibility within their organizations. This involves actively participating in meetings, volunteering for high-profile projects, and ensuring their achievements are recognized and attributed correctly. Being assertive about one's contributions and capabilities helps counteract biases that might undermine women's professional accomplishments.

Documentation and Feedback

Keeping detailed records of one's work performance, feedback received, and interactions that may reflect bias is crucial. This documentation can be invaluable during performance reviews or in situations where a person needs to demonstrate their achievements or challenge unfair treatment. Additionally, providing feedback about bias to the appropriate parties in a constructive manner can initiate important conversations that might lead to organizational change.

Legal Understanding and Advocacy

Understanding the legal framework regarding discrimination and bias is important. In many countries, there are laws designed to protect employees from discrimination based on gender, race, age, and other factors. Being informed about these rights can empower women to advocate for themselves and others effectively.

Promoting Inclusive Policies

Women in leadership positions, or those who have the ear of leadership, can advocate for the adoption and enforcement of inclusive policies. These might include unbiased hiring practices, transparent promotion pathways, and equitable pay structures. Policies that explicitly address and aim to reduce bias can create a more level playing field for all employees.

Developing Resilience and Seeking Professional Growth

Personal resilience is also critical in overcoming biases. This includes maintaining one's professional focus and integrity in the face of challenges and seeking continuous professional development to enhance one's skills and qualifications. By focusing on growth and excellence, women can position themselves as undeniable assets to their organizations, making it harder for biases to limit their career progression.

Mentorship and Sponsorship

Mentorship and sponsorship are particularly powerful tools for overcoming bias. Mentors can provide guidance and support, while sponsors can advocate for a mentee's advancement within the organization. Both roles can help women navigate biased environments and achieve their career goals despite systemic barriers.

Facilitating Organizational Change

Finally, women can play a pivotal role in facilitating organizational change by participating in or leading diversity and inclusion initiatives. By shaping policies and cultivating a culture that values diversity, women can help create environments where biases are less likely to thrive.

Overcoming bias requires a multifaceted approach involving personal strategies, organizational change, and cultural shifts. By employing these tactics and advocating for systemic improvements, women can help create more equitable workplaces where everyone has the opportunity to succeed based on their merits. This not only benefits women but enhances the overall productivity, creativity, and effectiveness of organizations.

ᗞᗞᗞ

"Education does more than fill a mind with facts; it ignites a spark of leadership potential that can change the world."

❥❥❥

EIGHT

RESILIENCE: BOUNCING BACK FROM SETBACKS

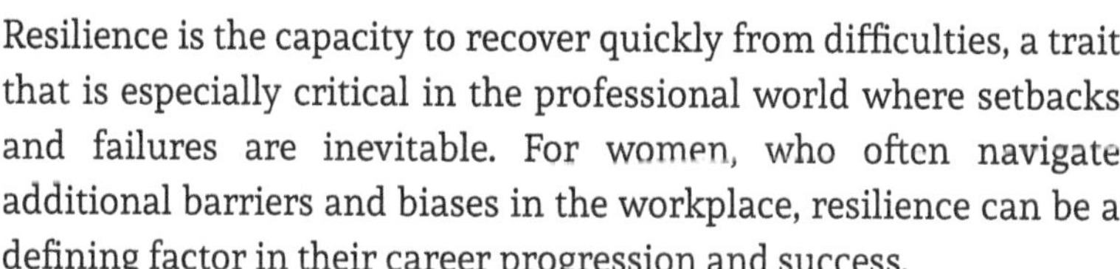

Resilience is the capacity to recover quickly from difficulties, a trait that is especially critical in the professional world where setbacks and failures are inevitable. For women, who often navigate additional barriers and biases in the workplace, resilience can be a defining factor in their career progression and success.

Understanding the Nature of Setbacks

Setbacks in a career can take various forms, ranging from missing out on a promotion or a project failing, to more personal losses like job redundancy or significant workplace conflict. Understanding that setbacks are a normal part of any career is crucial. They do not define professional capability but rather are opportunities for growth and learning.

The Importance of Resilience

Resilience is not about avoiding setbacks but rather about how one deals with challenges when they arise. It involves maintaining a level of steadiness and the ability to bounce back with more knowledge and experience. For women in leadership or those aspiring to lead, resilience is not just beneficial for individual careers but can also set a powerful example for teams and organizations.

Developing a Resilient Mindset

Cultivating a resilient mindset is foundational to managing and overcoming setbacks effectively. This mindset is characterized by adaptability, optimism, and an acceptance that setbacks are part of the journey. Developing such a mindset involves several key components:

Embracing a Growth Mindset

A growth mindset, a concept popularized by psychologist Carol Dweck, revolves around the belief that abilities and intelligence can be developed through dedication and hard work. This perspective encourages viewing challenges as opportunities to learn rather than insurmountable obstacles.

Staying Focused on Long-Term Goals

Resilient individuals keep their long-term goals in focus, which helps navigate through short-term setbacks. Keeping an eye on the ultimate objectives provides a sense of purpose and direction, aiding in overcoming immediate hurdles with greater ease.

Cultivating Emotional Intelligence

Emotional intelligence, the ability to identify, understand, manage, and use emotions positively, plays a significant role in resilience. High emotional intelligence helps in managing stress, communicating effectively, empathizing with others, overcoming challenges, and defusing conflict.

Strategies to Build Resilience

Building resilience is a proactive process. Women can adopt various strategies to strengthen their resilience in professional settings:

Develop Strong Support Networks

Having a robust support network, including peers, mentors, and family, can provide emotional backing and practical advice in times of need. Support networks can also offer different perspectives and help in brainstorming solutions to problems.

Maintain Physical and Mental Health

Physical health has a significant impact on mental resilience. Regular exercise, adequate sleep, and proper nutrition can enhance one's ability to cope with stress. Similarly, practices like mindfulness, meditation, and hobbies can maintain mental health and overall well-being.

Learn from Experiences

Every setback provides a learning opportunity. Analyzing what went wrong, what could be done differently, and how to prevent similar issues in the future can convert a negative experience into a valuable learning moment.

Be Flexible

Flexibility is a critical component of resilience. The ability to adapt to changing circumstances, modify plans, and shift strategies when necessary can make it much easier to navigate through setbacks.

Communicate Effectively

Open and effective communication can often prevent misunderstandings that might lead to setbacks. Moreover, when setbacks do occur, being able to communicate clearly can help in resolving issues more quickly and efficiently.

Seek Feedback

Feedback, both positive and negative, is invaluable for professional development. Seeking feedback can provide insights into areas of improvement and reaffirm strengths, helping to build resilience.

Practice Self-Compassion

Finally, it is essential for women to practice self-compassion. Being kind to oneself in the face of setbacks and acknowledging that perfection is unattainable can relieve some of the pressure that comes with professional roles.

Resilience is not an innate quality but a skill that can be developed over time. For women in the workforce, fostering resilience can make the difference between succumbing to the challenges and thriving despite them. By adopting these strategies, women can enhance their ability to bounce back from setbacks, paving the way for a robust, fulfilling, and successful career.

ᛈᛈᛈ

"The digital age has not just transformed how we work; it has revolutionized how women lead and influence across the globe."

ϷϷϷ

NINE

Innovation and Leadership: A Female Perspective

Innovation is a key driver of growth and success in today's rapidly changing business environment, and leadership plays a crucial role in fostering an innovative culture within organizations. When viewed through a female lens, innovation and leadership can take on unique characteristics influenced by diverse experiences, thought processes, and approaches. Women in leadership positions often bring fresh perspectives that challenge conventional methods and inspire creative solutions.

Understanding Innovation in Leadership

Innovation in leadership refers not only to the introduction of new products or technologies but also to new ways of thinking, problem-solving, and managing teams. It involves questioning the status quo, encouraging experimentation, and embracing the risks associated with trying something new. Leaders who innovate are not afraid to make decisions that could transform the business landscape and drive forward progress.

The Unique Contribution of Women to Innovative Leadership

Research suggests that companies with women in top management roles are more inclined towards innovation. Women's leadership styles, which often emphasize collaboration, empathy, and inclusivity, can contribute to more open and dynamic environments where creativity is encouraged and valued. Women are also more likely to value diverse perspectives and facilitate dialogue around different ideas, which are critical components of innovation.

Challenges Faced by Women in Innovative Leadership

Despite their potential to drive innovation, women often face specific challenges in leadership roles, especially in industries that are traditionally male-dominated. These challenges can include overcoming gender biases that question their capabilities in leadership and innovation, a lack of support networks that provide guidance and mentorship, and fewer role models who have navigated similar paths.

Strategies for Promoting Innovation as a Female Leader

Women can employ several strategies to enhance their effectiveness as innovative leaders:

Fostering an Inclusive Culture

Creating an environment where all team members feel valued and empowered to share their ideas is crucial. This includes encouraging participation from everyone, regardless of their position or background, and actively seeking input from those who might otherwise remain silent. An inclusive culture not only improves employee engagement but also leads to a richer pool of ideas, driving innovation.

Leveraging Emotional Intelligence

Women often score highly on measures of emotional intelligence, which includes skills like empathy, self-awareness, and social expertise. These skills can be leveraged to build strong relationships within and outside the organization, anticipate the needs and responses of both employees and customers, and create products or solutions that truly meet market demands.

Adopting a Flexible Approach to Problem-Solving

Innovation requires flexibility and a willingness to depart from traditional methods of thinking and doing business. Female leaders can use their typically strong skills in adaptability and multitasking to explore various solutions to problems, experimenting with new approaches that might not be immediately obvious.

Utilizing Collaborative Leadership Styles

Women often adopt a collaborative approach to leadership. This style can be particularly effective in fostering innovation as it involves team members in the decision-making process and makes use of collective intelligence to refine ideas and solutions.

Committing to Lifelong Learning

The landscape of innovation is constantly evolving, with new technologies and theories developing all the time. Committing to lifelong learning—whether through formal education, self-study, or professional development activities—ensures that female leaders can stay at the cutting edge of their industries.

Networking and Alliance Building

Building a broad network can provide access to new ideas, technologies, and methodologies. Networks can also offer support and resources for implementing innovative ideas. Women in leadership positions should seek to build alliances both within their industries and in other fields to enhance their innovative capacities.

Championing Risk-Taking

Innovation often involves risk. Women leaders can cultivate a risk-tolerant environment by promoting smart risk-taking and viewing failures as learning opportunities. Encouraging teams to experiment and take calculated risks can lead to breakthrough innovations.

Driving Organizational Change

As leaders, women have the opportunity to drive change within their organizations. This can mean pushing for new policies that promote innovation, such as investing in research and development, providing time and resources for team members to pursue creative projects, or adopting new technologies that disrupt traditional business processes.

Women bring distinct strengths to leadership that can significantly enhance the innovative capacities of their organizations. By embracing and fostering a culture of innovation, leveraging their inherent skills, and actively promoting inclusive and collaborative environments, female leaders can drive significant advancements in their industries. Their unique perspectives and approaches can lead to innovative solutions that not only propel businesses forward but also contribute to a more balanced and equitable corporate landscape.

ppp

"Workplace policies that support women are not just about facilitating balance; they are about recognizing and harnessing the true value of diversity."

ppp

TEN

EDUCATION AND EMPOWERMENT: TOOLS FOR SUCCESS

Education and empowerment serve as critical tools for the success and advancement of women in all spheres of life, particularly in their professional careers. These tools provide the foundation for breaking barriers, achieving economic independence, and assuming leadership roles. The role of education in empowering women is multifaceted, encompassing formal education, continuous learning, and personal development, all of which contribute significantly to a woman's ability to navigate and excel in her career.

The Link Between Education and Professional Success

Education opens doors to better career opportunities. For women, this link is especially crucial because educational qualifications can help overcome some of the systemic barriers to entry into higher-paying and more prestigious careers. Higher education levels are strongly correlated with higher employment rates, greater earnings, and more substantial positions of leadership within companies and organizations.

Overcoming Barriers Through Education

Despite progress in educational attainment for women, several barriers still exist that can hinder their full educational and subsequent professional participation. These include societal expectations, economic constraints, and the underrepresentation of women in certain fields, especially in STEM (Science, Technology, Engineering, and Mathematics) and leadership positions. Addressing these barriers involves not only providing access to education but also ensuring that educational environments are inclusive and supportive of women's needs and aspirations.

Strategies for Enhancing Education and Empowerment

Expanding Access to Education

One of the most direct ways to empower women is by expanding their access to education. This includes not only formal education but also vocational training and non-traditional educational pathways that can lead to lucrative and fulfilling careers. Scholarships, financial aid, and educational programs targeted at women, particularly those from disadvantaged backgrounds, can play a significant role in expanding access.

Promoting STEM Education for Women

Encouraging more women to enter STEM fields is a critical aspect of empowerment. This can be achieved by introducing young girls to STEM subjects in fun and engaging ways, mentoring programs that connect women with leaders in these fields, and by combating stereotypes that suggest these subjects are more suited to men.

Lifelong Learning and Professional Development

Empowerment through education doesn't end with formal schooling. Lifelong learning and continual professional development are crucial as the job market evolves and new technologies emerge. Opportunities for ongoing education, such as workshops, seminars, certifications, and online courses, allow women to continually upgrade their skills and remain competitive in the workforce.

Building Soft Skills

While technical skills are important, soft skills such as communication, leadership, negotiation, and problem-solving are equally vital. These skills empower women to navigate workplace dynamics effectively, assume leadership roles, and advocate for themselves and others. Training programs focused on these areas can enhance women's professional profiles and open up new opportunities for advancement.

Using Education to Challenge Cultural Norms

Education also plays a transformative role in challenging and changing cultural norms that limit women's roles in society. By promoting gender equality and women's rights within educational content and fostering an environment that supports girls and young women, educational institutions can become catalysts for cultural change.

Networking and Mentorship

Education can be significantly enhanced by opportunities for networking and mentorship. These relationships provide women with guidance, expose them to new opportunities, and offer support systems that can be crucial for navigating challenges in their careers and personal lives.

Empowerment through Leadership Training

Specific training in leadership can empower women to take on leadership roles with confidence. Leadership training programs designed for women can address unique challenges women face, such as managing work-life balance, leading with empathy, and overcoming implicit biases in the workplace.

The Role of Policy and Advocacy

Finally, advocating for policies that support women's education and empowerment is essential. This includes policies that ensure equal access to education, protect against discrimination in educational and professional environments, and promote work-life balance through supportive workplace practices.

Education and empowerment are interlinked tools that provide women with the knowledge, skills, and confidence to succeed professionally and personally. By investing in women's education and supporting their empowerment through various strategies, societies can unlock a tremendous source of innovation, leadership, and productivity that benefits everyone.

ᛝᛝᛝ

"*Effective negotiation by women isn't about claiming victory; it's about crafting outcomes where everyone feels valued and heard.*"

ᗡᗡᗡ

ELEVEN

COMMUNICATION STYLES: ASSERTIVENESS VS. AGGRESSIVENESS

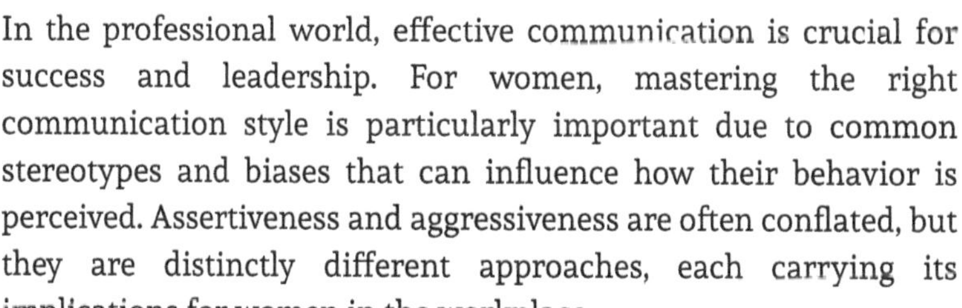

In the professional world, effective communication is crucial for success and leadership. For women, mastering the right communication style is particularly important due to common stereotypes and biases that can influence how their behavior is perceived. Assertiveness and aggressiveness are often conflated, but they are distinctly different approaches, each carrying its implications for women in the workplace.

Understanding Assertiveness and Aggressiveness

Assertiveness is a communication style characterized by confidence and directness in expressing one's thoughts, feelings, and needs without undermining the rights of others. It is about being forthright about your wants and needs, while still considering and respecting the perspectives and wishes of others. Aggressiveness, on the other hand, involves expressing one's thoughts and feelings in a way that violates the rights of others. This might include dominating conversations, dismissing other people's ideas, or even verbal attacks.

The Double Bind for Women

Women often face what is known as a "double bind" in communication. If they are too assertive, they risk being labeled as aggressive or unfeminine, which can harm their professional reputation and advancement. If they are not assertive enough, they may be seen as weak or ineffective leaders. Finding the right balance in communication style is therefore not just a matter of personal expression, but a strategic necessity.

Strategies for Assertive Communication

Developing an assertive communication style involves several key elements:

Clarity and Directness

Being clear and direct involves straightforwardly expressing your thoughts, needs, and desires without being ambiguous. This means being specific about what you want and expect without leaving much room for misunderstanding. It also involves the ability to say 'no' when necessary, setting and maintaining personal boundaries.

Active Listening

Assertive communication isn't just about expressing one's own opinions; it also involves listening actively to others. This means truly hearing what others are saying, asking clarifying questions, and responding thoughtfully. Active listening can help in building rapport and trust, essential components of effective leadership.

Maintaining Composure

Assertiveness requires maintaining one's composure, even in difficult conversations. Keeping emotions in check, using a calm tone, and choosing words carefully are all part of this. It helps in keeping the conversation constructive and prevents it from escalating into conflict.

Using "I" Statements

"I" statements are a powerful tool in assertive communication. By framing your statements around your own experiences and feelings rather than attributing intentions or faults to others, you can express your point of view more openly and honestly without making others feel defensive or attacked.

Nonverbal Communication

Nonverbal cues play a significant role in communication. Maintaining eye contact, using appropriate facial expressions, and keeping your posture open and engaged are all important in conveying confidence and respect.

Handling Aggressiveness

In situations where a woman is perceived as aggressive rather than assertive, it is crucial to step back and evaluate the communication style and the perceptions of others. Reflection on feedback, whether formal or informal, can provide insights into how communication is being received and what adjustments may be necessary.

Adapting Communication Styles

Different situations may require different communication approaches. For instance, a more directive style might be necessary in a crisis, while a collaborative approach might be better suited for team-building activities. Being flexible and adapting your style to the context can enhance effectiveness and perception.

The Impact of Assertive Communication

Assertive communication can lead to better outcomes in negotiations, conflict resolution, and team leadership. It fosters an environment of openness and mutual respect, where ideas can flow freely, and innovation can thrive. For women, mastering assertiveness can be particularly empowering, helping to navigate the fine line between passivity and aggressiveness and enhancing their leadership presence.

Understanding and practicing assertive communication can significantly impact a woman's professional journey. By distinguishing assertiveness from aggressiveness and applying effective communication strategies, women can assert their leadership, influence outcomes, and contribute positively to their workplaces, paving the way for a more balanced and respectful professional environment.

ᗡᗡᗡ

"Sustainable leadership is not measured by short-term achievements but by the long-term health and impact of both the community and the environment."

ᑭᑭᑭ

TWELVE

LEADERSHIP STYLES: THE FEMININE APPROACH

The concept of leadership has evolved significantly over the years, particularly with more women ascending to positions of power across various sectors. This shift has brought increased attention to what is often termed the "feminine approach" to leadership. This approach doesn't solely refer to a style adopted by women but to a broader, more inclusive leadership style characterized by traits and values traditionally categorized as feminine. These include empathy, inclusivity, collaborative problem-solving, and emotional intelligence.

Defining Feminine Leadership

Feminine leadership emphasizes qualities such as empathy, nurturing, and cooperation—traits that have been undervalued in traditional leadership paradigms but are increasingly recognized as essential for leading modern organizations. This style is contrasted with the more traditional masculine leadership style, which often emphasizes assertiveness, competitiveness, and control. Feminine leadership does not seek to replace masculine traits but to integrate both to create a more balanced leadership approach.

The Benefits of Feminine Leadership

Research suggests that organizations led by individuals who embrace feminine leadership traits often experience a range of benefits, including improved employee satisfaction, higher levels of creativity and innovation, and better problem-solving capabilities. Here's how these traits translate into effective leadership practices:

Empathy and Emotional Intelligence

One of the cornerstones of feminine leadership is a high level of emotional intelligence, which includes the ability to empathize with others. Leaders who can understand and relate to the feelings of their team members are better equipped to manage personnel issues, motivate their staff, and create a supportive work environment that values each member's contributions.

Collaboration Over Competition

Feminine leadership often prioritizes collaboration over competition. This approach fosters team cohesion and leverages the diverse strengths of all team members to achieve common goals. By encouraging an atmosphere where ideas are freely shared, leaders can harness the collective intelligence of the group.

Flexibility and Adaptability

Adaptability is another significant aspect of feminine leadership. Leaders who embrace this style are often more open to change and new ideas, adapting their strategies to meet evolving circumstances and challenges. This flexibility can be particularly advantageous in times of uncertainty or rapid market changes.

Inclusivity and Diversity

Inclusive leadership is integral to the feminine approach. This style values diverse perspectives and backgrounds, integrating them into decision-making processes to enhance creativity and innovation. Leaders who are inclusive not only contribute to a fairer and more equitable workplace but also tap into a wider range of experiences and ideas, driving better business outcomes.

Transformational Leadership

Feminine leadership is closely aligned with transformational leadership, which involves inspiring and motivating followers to exceed their own self-interests for the good of the group and to perform beyond their perceived capabilities. This leadership style is characterized by setting high expectations and then supporting followers to meet these expectations through coaching, feedback, and recognition of individual contributions.

Challenges Facing Feminine Leadership

Despite its benefits, feminine leadership can face challenges, especially in environments that have historically valued and rewarded more masculine approaches. Leaders using a feminine style may struggle with being perceived as too soft or not authoritative enough, particularly in high-stakes or traditionally male-dominated industries.

Strategies for Effective Feminine Leadership

To maximize the effectiveness of a feminine leadership approach, leaders can adopt several strategies:

Communicate Clearly and Assertively

Effective communication is key. Leaders should be clear and assertive in their communications, ensuring that their kindness or empathy is not mistaken for weakness or indecision.

Build Strong Networks

Strong professional networks can provide support, foster opportunities for growth, and offer a platform for sharing challenges and strategies. These networks can be particularly valuable for women in leadership roles, providing both support and validation.

Leverage Mentorship

Both providing and receiving mentorship can be incredibly beneficial. Leaders can develop their skills and strategies while helping others to grow, creating a cycle of empowerment and improvement.

Seek Continuous Feedback

Feedback is crucial for any leader's development. Openness to feedback can help leaders refine their approach and make necessary adjustments to their style and strategies.

The feminine approach to leadership offers a powerful and increasingly relevant model in today's complex, interconnected world. By blending traditionally feminine traits with more conventional leadership qualities, leaders can create more adaptable, inclusive, and effective organizations. This approach not only enhances the work environment but also drives sustainable success in the modern business landscape.

DR. MINAKSHI BANSAL

❧❧❧

"Women's leadership is not a trend; it is a
transformative force that is reshaping the
landscape of power in every sector."

💗💗💗

THIRTEEN

BUILDING YOUR PERSONAL BRAND AS A WOMAN LEADER

In today's competitive landscape, developing a personal brand is crucial for anyone looking to advance their career, especially for women in leadership roles. A strong personal brand helps to establish a leader's identity, differentiate them from their peers, and communicate their values, strengths, and unique capabilities. For women, this can be particularly powerful in overcoming gender stereotypes and establishing credibility in traditionally male-dominated environments.

Understanding Personal Branding

Personal branding involves creating a distinct and consistent image and reputation that others recognize and associate with you. This goes beyond just professional skills; it encompasses your entire persona, including how you communicate, your leadership style, your values, and your professional accomplishments. A well-crafted personal brand makes you memorable and can significantly influence your career trajectory by opening up opportunities for promotions, speaking engagements, and broader professional recognition.

Steps to Build a Strong Personal Brand

Define Your Unique Value Proposition

Begin by defining what makes you unique. What are your core strengths and values? How do these contribute to your professional identity? Identifying your unique value proposition involves a deep understanding of your personal and professional goals and how you can offer solutions to challenges within your industry or organization.

Align Your Public Image With Your Personal Values

Consistency is key in personal branding. Ensure that your public persona, including your online presence, public speeches, and interactions, consistently reflects your personal values and professional strengths. This consistency helps to reinforce your brand and makes you more recognizable.

Leverage Social Media Platforms

Social media is a powerful tool for building and maintaining your personal brand. Platforms like LinkedIn, Twitter, and even Instagram offer opportunities to share your professional insights, celebrate your accomplishments, and connect with others in your field. Regularly posting relevant content, engaging with others' posts, and contributing to discussions can help solidify your presence in your industry.

Engage in Thought Leadership

One of the most effective ways to build your personal brand is to position yourself as a thought leader. This can be achieved through blogging, publishing articles, speaking at conferences, and participating in panels. Sharing your expertise not only enhances your credibility but also expands your professional network.

Network Strategically

Networking is more than just collecting contacts—it's about building meaningful relationships that are mutually beneficial. Attend industry conferences, join professional organizations, and participate in workshops and seminars. Each interaction is an opportunity to present your personal brand and forge new connections that could lead to future opportunities.

Seek Visibility in Your Field

Visibility is crucial in establishing and growing your personal brand. Seek out opportunities within and outside your organization to showcase your skills and leadership. This could be leading a high-profile project, volunteering for committee roles, or participating in community services. Each of these activities can increase your visibility and strengthen your personal brand.

Cultivate Professional Relationships

Building strong relationships with other professionals can enhance your brand. Mentors, peers, and even competitors can provide valuable feedback, endorse your skills, and recommend you for opportunities. A strong network also serves as a platform to demonstrate your leadership skills and industry knowledge.

Manage Your Online Reputation

In the digital age, managing your online reputation is vital. Regularly monitor your presence on the internet, update your professional profiles, and ensure that your content is appropriate and aligns with your brand. Tools like Google alerts can help you keep track of where and how your name is mentioned online.

Practice Consistent Communication

Every communication should reflect your personal brand, from the way you write emails to how you conduct yourself in meetings. Being consistent in your communication style helps reinforce who you are and what you stand for.

Continuously Evaluate and Adapt Your Brand

Finally, personal branding is not a one-time effort but an ongoing process. Regularly reflect on your brand's effectiveness and make adjustments as necessary. As your career evolves, so too should your brand, adapting to new roles, challenges, and shifts in your professional life.

Building a personal brand as a woman leader involves understanding your unique value, consistently projecting this value through various channels, and maintaining a reputation that aligns with your professional goals and personal values. Through strategic personal branding, women leaders can establish a strong presence in their fields, influence others, and pave the way for further professional opportunities and achievements.

ᖰᖰᖰ

"The future of women in leadership is not just promising—it's essential for a balanced and equitable global society."

▷▷▷

FOURTEEN

SOCIAL MEDIA AND LEADERSHIP: HARNESSING THE POWER OF DIGITAL PLATFORMS

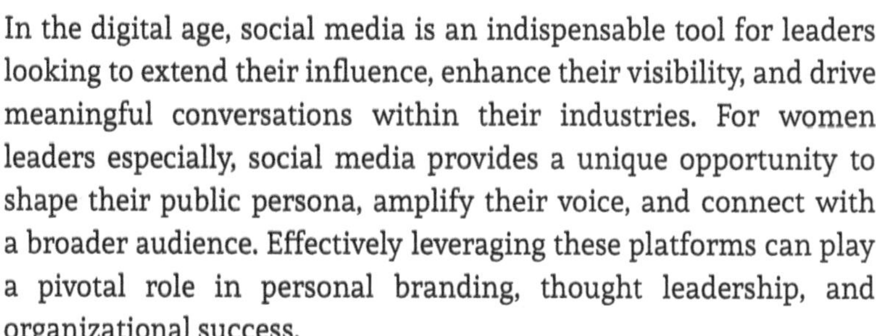

In the digital age, social media is an indispensable tool for leaders looking to extend their influence, enhance their visibility, and drive meaningful conversations within their industries. For women leaders especially, social media provides a unique opportunity to shape their public persona, amplify their voice, and connect with a broader audience. Effectively leveraging these platforms can play a pivotal role in personal branding, thought leadership, and organizational success.

Understanding the Impact of Social Media on Leadership

Social media has transformed the landscape of leadership by democratizing the spread of information and allowing leaders to engage directly with their audience. This direct line of communication can be used to influence public opinion, share insights, promote initiatives, and build a community around shared values and objectives. For leaders, social media is not just a marketing tool; it is a strategic asset that can enhance their ability to lead and inspire.

Building a Social Media Strategy for Leaders

To harness the power of social media effectively, leaders should consider the following strategies:

Define Clear Objectives

Before diving into social media, it's important for leaders to define what they aim to achieve. Objectives can range from building brand awareness and networking to thought leadership or advocacy for specific causes. Clear objectives will help tailor content strategies and measure the success of social media efforts.

Choose the Right Platforms

Not all social media platforms are suitable for every purpose. LinkedIn, for example, is ideal for professional networking and content sharing, while Twitter is great for quick updates and engaging in industry-related conversations. Instagram or YouTube might be more effective for storytelling or visual content. Choosing the right platforms depends on where a leader's audience spends their time and the type of content they are likely to consume.

Create Quality Content

Content is at the heart of any social media strategy. For leaders, content should not only reflect their expertise but also their personality and leadership philosophy. This could include articles, blogs, video messages, podcasts, or infographics. Quality content should provide value, provoke thought, and encourage engagement from followers.

Engage Authentically

Engagement is key to building and maintaining a strong social media presence. This means not only posting content but also interacting with followers, responding to comments, and participating in conversations. Authentic engagement helps build trust and loyalty among followers and can enhance a leader's reputation as accessible and responsive.

Maintain Consistency

Consistency in posting frequency and messaging helps in building a dependable presence. Followers come to expect regular updates and consistent themes, which can enhance a leader's credibility and reliability. Tools like content calendars and scheduling software can help maintain this consistency.

Monitor and Adapt

Social media is dynamic, and what works today might not work tomorrow. Leaders need to continuously monitor the performance of their social media activities and be ready to adapt their strategies based on what the data shows. This might involve tweaking the type of content, adjusting posting schedules, or even shifting focus to different platforms.

Leverage Social Media for Crisis Management

Social media can be an effective tool for crisis management. By providing timely updates and addressing issues head-on, leaders can mitigate negative impacts and demonstrate their responsiveness. Transparent and honest communication during a crisis can enhance a leader's reputation for integrity and accountability.

Promote Diversity and Inclusion

Leaders can use social media to promote diversity and inclusion within their industries. By sharing stories of diverse team members, supporting inclusive projects, and advocating for equality, leaders can use their platforms to influence positive change and build a culture of inclusivity.

Personalize Your Presence

While maintaining professionalism, it's also beneficial for leaders to show aspects of their personal lives or personalities. This humanizes them and makes them more relatable to their audience. Sharing personal insights, experiences, or even challenges can foster a deeper connection with followers.

Social media offers leaders a powerful suite of tools to enhance their visibility, influence public discourse, and lead more effectively in the digital age. By crafting a thoughtful strategy that emphasizes quality content, authentic engagement, and consistent messaging, leaders can maximize the benefits of these digital platforms and position themselves at the forefront of their fields.

ppp

"Empathy in leadership is not a weakness but a
formidable strength, allowing leaders to forge
connections that turn challenges into triumphs."

ᐅᐅᐅ

FIFTEEN

WORKPLACE POLICIES THAT SUPPORT WOMEN

Creating an inclusive and supportive work environment is essential for the advancement and retention of women in the workforce. Effective workplace policies that support women not only help in balancing work and personal life but also play a crucial role in fostering equal opportunities for career progression. Such policies are not just beneficial for women but enhance the overall productivity and satisfaction of all employees by creating a more supportive and equitable workplace.

Family-Friendly Policies

One of the key areas where workplace policies can support women is in facilitating a balance between work and family commitments. Family-friendly policies include:

Paid Parental Leave: Extending paid leave to both mothers and fathers encourages shared responsibility for child-rearing and supports women in maintaining their careers after childbirth.

Flexible Working Hours: Policies allowing flexible work hours or compressed workweeks can help employees manage family and work responsibilities more effectively.

Remote Work Options: Allowing employees to work from home or remotely provides flexibility and can be particularly beneficial for mothers.

Childcare Support: Providing onsite childcare, subsidies for external childcare services, or resources to find suitable childcare can remove significant barriers for working mothers.

Equal Pay and Career Advancement

Another critical area for policy development is in ensuring equal pay for equal work and supporting the career advancement of women:

Transparent Pay Policies: Implementing clear and transparent pay scales that ensure equal pay for equal work helps to eliminate the gender pay gap.

Career Development Programs: Initiatives such as mentoring programs, leadership training, and sponsorship can help women advance in their careers.

Succession Planning: Including women in succession planning for senior roles ensures that gender diversity is considered in leadership progression.

Anti-Discrimination and Harassment Policies

To create a safe and respectful workplace, robust anti-discrimination and harassment policies must be in place:

Zero Tolerance Policy: A strict zero-tolerance policy against all forms of harassment and discrimination should be clearly communicated to all employees.

Regular Training: Conducting regular training sessions on diversity, inclusion, and sensitivity training can help in reducing incidents of discrimination and harassment.

Reporting Mechanisms: Safe, confidential, and accessible reporting mechanisms should be available to employees to report any incidents without fear of retaliation.

Health and Well-being

Supporting the health and well-being of employees is vital, and women often face specific health issues:

Healthcare Benefits: Comprehensive health benefits that cover reproductive health, mental health services, and preventive care are crucial.

Support for Menstrual and Menopausal Health: Policies that acknowledge and support women during menstruation and menopause, such as flexible sick leave, can create a supportive environment.

Well-being Programs: Programs that promote overall well-being, including access to fitness centers, yoga classes, and mental health days, support a healthy work-life balance.

Inclusive Culture and Diversity

Promoting an inclusive culture and diversity within the workplace is essential for supporting women:

Diversity and Inclusion Initiatives: These initiatives should aim to foster an inclusive culture where all employees feel valued and included.

Employee Resource Groups: Support groups for women and other minority groups can provide a platform for sharing experiences and support.

Regular Reviews: Conducting regular reviews of workplace culture and policies to ensure they meet the diverse needs of all employees.

Support During Life Transitions

Women often face various life transitions that can impact their career progression:

Support for Pregnant Employees: Policies that support pregnant women, such as prenatal care leave or appointments during work hours, are important.

Return-to-Work Programs: After extended leaves, return-to-work programs can help women reintegrate into the workplace more smoothly.

Career Break Programs: Policies that allow for career breaks for personal or family reasons without losing career traction can be incredibly beneficial.

Implementing and regularly updating these policies ensure that the workplace is supportive and equitable for women. These policies not only help in attracting and retaining female talent but also contribute to a more diverse, innovative, and productive organizational culture. By prioritizing the support of women through comprehensive workplace policies, organizations can significantly enhance their competitiveness and reputation as employers of choice.

❦❦❦

• 91 •

"Inclusivity in leadership does more than fill quotas—it builds stronger, more creative, and more resilient organizations."

❦❦❦

SIXTEEN
NEGOTIATION TECHNIQUES FOR WOMEN IN LEADERSHIP

Negotiation is a critical skill for any leader, essential for navigating contracts, salaries, budgets, and team dynamics. However, for women in leadership, mastering negotiation techniques can be particularly challenging due to enduring stereotypes and biases that might influence the perception of their assertiveness or decisiveness. Effective negotiation strategies tailored for women can empower them to advocate for themselves and their teams more effectively, ensuring fair outcomes and advancing their leadership roles.

Understanding the Landscape

Women often face unique challenges in negotiation scenarios, including the double bind of being perceived as either too soft or too aggressive. Historical gender roles can lead to unconscious biases, affecting how women's negotiation tactics are received compared to their male counterparts. Acknowledging these challenges is the first step in developing effective strategies to overcome them.

Key Negotiation Techniques for Women Leaders

Preparation is Key

Thorough preparation is the cornerstone of successful negotiation. This involves understanding all aspects of the negotiation, including the needs, wants, and limits of both sides. Women leaders should gather as much information as possible about the people involved and the context of the negotiation to anticipate objections and plan responses. Setting clear goals for what needs to be achieved in the negotiation can also help in steering discussions effectively.

Build Rapport

Establishing a connection with the negotiating party can create a more cooperative environment and facilitate easier agreement. Women can leverage their typically strong interpersonal skills to build rapport. This might involve small talk, finding common interests, or expressing empathy towards the challenges faced by the other party. Building rapport doesn't just make negotiations smoother; it also helps in creating long-term relationships that can be beneficial in future interactions.

Assertiveness with Diplomacy

Being assertive is about clearly and confidently expressing needs and wants without aggression. Women in leadership can practice assertive communication by using direct language, maintaining steady eye contact, and keeping a firm but polite tone. Balancing assertiveness with diplomacy ensures that negotiations are constructive and that all parties feel respected throughout the process.

Use of Collaborative Language

Framing negotiation points in a way that highlights mutual benefits is a powerful technique. Using collaborative language can help in shifting the negotiation from a win-lose scenario to a win-win outcome. For example, phrases like "Let's see how we can both benefit from this arrangement" can encourage more cooperative discussions and lead to solutions that address the needs of all parties involved.

Emphasize Value

Women should articulate the value they bring to the table clearly and confidently. This involves not just stating what they want but also why they deserve it and how it benefits the organization or project. This is particularly important in salary negotiations or discussions of project funding, where demonstrating the direct impact of one's work on organizational goals is crucial.

Practice Active Listening

Effective negotiators are also attentive listeners. Active listening involves paying close attention to what the other party is saying, asking clarifying questions, and reflecting back what you have heard to ensure understanding. This not only helps in gathering valuable information but also makes the other party feel respected and heard, which can facilitate more open discussions.

Manage Emotions

Negotiations can sometimes become tense or confrontational. Managing emotions effectively ensures that decisions are made rationally rather than reactively. Techniques such as taking deep breaths, pausing before responding, and maintaining a calm demeanor can help in managing one's own emotions and de-escalating conflicts should they arise.

Seek Win-Win Outcomes

The goal of negotiation should not always be to 'win' at the expense of the other but to find solutions that benefit both sides. This mindset can lead to more creative solutions and more sustainable agreements. It also builds a positive reputation over time, making future negotiations easier and more productive.

Know When to Walk Away

Understanding one's limits and being willing to walk away from a negotiation if it doesn't meet the minimum acceptable criteria is crucial. This not only preserves one's own interests but also sends a strong message about one's negotiation position and self-worth.

Continual Improvement

Finally, negotiation is a skill that can be continuously improved. Seeking feedback, reflecting on past negotiations, and ongoing training can help women leaders enhance their negotiation skills over time.

Mastering these negotiation techniques enables women leaders to navigate complex discussions effectively, advocate for their needs and the needs of their teams, and achieve outcomes that reflect their true value and contributions. By adopting a strategic approach to negotiation, women can strengthen their leadership influence and pave the way for more equitable and effective organizational dynamics.

❧❧❧

"The path to leadership for women is often a
complex journey of navigating biases, breaking
barriers, and setting new precedents for success and
integrity."

ᚦᚦᚦ

SEVENTEEN

SUSTAINABILITY AND ETHICS IN LEADERSHIP

In today's business environment, sustainability and ethics are not just optional; they are essential components of responsible leadership. Leaders who prioritize these elements are better equipped to build trust with stakeholders, achieve long-term organizational goals, and positively impact society and the environment. This focus is particularly critical as consumers, employees, and investors increasingly demand transparency, ethical operations, and sustainable practices from organizations.

Understanding Sustainability and Ethics in Leadership

Sustainability in leadership refers to practices and strategies that not only ensure the current viability of the organization but also consider long-term impacts on the environment and society. Ethical leadership, on the other hand, involves making decisions that are not only legally compliant but also morally right, fostering a culture of fairness, integrity, and respect.

The Importance of Ethical Leadership

Ethical leadership is foundational for building credibility and maintaining a good reputation. It involves leading by example, where leaders demonstrate commitment to ethical behavior in their actions and decision-making processes. This commitment helps to instill a corporate culture that values integrity over short-term gains, which is crucial for sustainable success.

Integrating Sustainability into Business Practices

Leaders can integrate sustainability into their business practices by:

Developing Sustainable Products and Services: This involves designing products and services that minimize environmental impact, are made from sustainable materials, and can be recycled or reused at the end of their lifecycle.

Implementing Sustainable Operations: Leaders should look to reduce waste, increase energy efficiency, and utilize renewable energy sources in their operations to decrease the environmental footprint of their organization.

Engaging in Responsible Sourcing: This includes choosing suppliers who adhere to ethical labor practices and have environmentally friendly operations, thereby extending the organization's commitment to sustainability through its supply chain.

Promoting a Culture of Ethical Behavior

To foster a culture of ethical behavior, leaders must:

Set Clear Ethical Standards: Establishing and communicating clear ethical guidelines that outline expected behaviors and the handling of various business scenarios is crucial. These guidelines should be integrated into all levels of the organization.

Provide Ethics Training: Regular training sessions on ethics can help reinforce the organization's commitment to integrity and ensure that all employees understand their ethical obligations.

Encourage Open Communication: Creating an environment where employees feel safe to report unethical behavior without fear of retaliation is essential for maintaining ethical standards.

Ethical Decision-Making

Ethical decision-making involves considering the broader impact of business decisions on all stakeholders, including employees, customers, communities, and the environment. This may include:

Considering Long-Term Impacts: Ethical leaders think beyond short-term profitability to consider how decisions will affect stakeholders in the long run.

Balancing Stakeholder Interests: Striving to balance the competing needs and interests of different stakeholder groups in decision-making processes.

Being Transparent: Maintaining transparency with stakeholders about business operations and the decision-making process builds trust and demonstrates integrity.

Sustainability Reporting

Transparency in sustainability efforts can be achieved through regular sustainability reporting, where organizations disclose their environmental and social impacts. This transparency not only holds the organization accountable but also builds trust with stakeholders.

Leadership Accountability

Leaders must hold themselves and their organizations accountable for their impacts on society and the environment. This can be facilitated by:

Setting Measurable Sustainability Goals: Clear, measurable goals allow organizations to track their progress and make adjustments as needed.

Conducting Regular Audits: Regular audits of both sustainability practices and ethical behavior help ensure compliance and identify areas for improvement.

Engaging Stakeholders: Regular engagement with stakeholders can provide insights into how the organization's practices affect them and offer ideas for how to improve.

Challenges in Ethical and Sustainable Leadership

Despite the benefits, ethical and sustainable leadership can present challenges, including higher initial costs, resistance to change within the organization, and the complexity of implementing comprehensive ethical and sustainable practices. Overcoming these challenges requires strong commitment from leadership, clear communication of the benefits, and a willingness to invest in long-term gains.

Sustainability and ethics are increasingly recognized as critical elements of effective leadership. Leaders who embrace these principles can drive their organizations to not only achieve financial success but also contribute positively to society and the environment, creating a lasting legacy that extends beyond the bottom line. By prioritizing ethical behavior and sustainable practices, leaders can build stronger, more resilient organizations that are well-equipped to face the challenges of the modern world.

"Health and well-being are the bedrock upon which
women leaders build their capacity to innovate,
influence, and inspire."

❥❥❥

EIGHTEEN

HEALTH AND WELL-BEING FOR THE FEMALE LEADER

Health and well-being are critical for anyone looking to succeed in demanding roles, and for female leaders, the stakes can be particularly high. The unique challenges faced by women in leadership positions—ranging from managing workplace stress to balancing professional and personal responsibilities—make prioritizing their health and well-being essential not just for personal success, but for the broader influence they have within their organizations and communities.

Understanding the Health Challenges for Female Leaders

Female leaders often juggle multiple roles both at work and at home, which can lead to increased stress levels, burnout, and health problems. The pressure to perform consistently at a high level, often in environments that may still harbor subtle biases, adds another layer of stress. Recognizing these unique challenges is the first step toward addressing them effectively.

Strategies for Maintaining Health and Well-being

To manage these pressures and maintain health and well-being, female leaders can adopt several effective strategies:

Regular Physical Activity

Engaging in regular physical activity is one of the most effective ways to reduce stress and improve overall health. Exercise releases endorphins, which have mood-lifting properties, and helps in maintaining cardiovascular health, strength, and flexibility. Whether it's yoga, running, or strength training, finding an activity that is enjoyable and fits into a busy schedule is key.

Balanced Nutrition

Eating a balanced diet is essential for maintaining energy levels and overall health. For busy leaders, planning meals ahead and choosing whole, nutrient-dense foods can help sustain energy throughout long days and reduce the temptation to rely on quick, unhealthy options. Staying hydrated is also crucial, as even mild dehydration can affect cognitive function and energy levels.

Adequate Sleep

Sleep is often the first thing sacrificed by busy professionals. However, inadequate sleep can impair cognitive function, decision-making, and even emotional regulation. Female leaders should prioritize getting enough sleep—typically 7-9 hours per night—to ensure they are operating at their best.

Stress Management Techniques

Effective stress management is crucial for long-term health and career sustainability. Techniques such as mindfulness meditation, deep breathing exercises, or even short breaks during the day can be highly effective. Regular practice can help manage stress levels and improve overall mental well-being.

Mental Health Care

Mental health is as important as physical health. Accessing professional help when needed—such as talking therapies or counseling—can be vital in managing mental health challenges. Leaders should not hesitate to seek support for issues like anxiety, depression, or burnout.

Setting Boundaries

One key aspect of maintaining well-being is setting and enforcing boundaries between work and personal life. This can mean making time for family and hobbies, or simply ensuring that there are times when work is put aside. Technology can help by setting reminders to take breaks or by using features that limit notifications outside of work hours.

Building a Support Network

Having a robust support network can make a significant difference in a leader's ability to manage stress and maintain well-being. This network can include family, friends, professional mentors, and peers who understand the unique pressures of leadership roles.

Regular Health Check-Ups

Preventative healthcare is crucial. Regular check-ups can catch potential health issues before they become serious, and routine screenings are essential for early detection of conditions common in women, such as breast and cervical cancer.

Personal Development and Lifelong Learning

Continual personal and professional development can contribute positively to a leader's sense of purpose and self-esteem. Engaging in lifelong learning—whether related to professional skills, personal interests, or other areas—can enhance mental agility and provide a refreshing counterpoint to daily work-related challenges.

Practicing Gratitude and Reflection

Maintaining a practice of gratitude and reflection can improve mental health and overall life satisfaction. Taking time to reflect on successes, learning from failures, and expressing gratitude for both can foster a positive mindset and resilience.

Incorporating these strategies into daily routines can help female leaders not only manage the demands of their roles but also thrive. Prioritizing health and well-being ultimately enhances leadership effectiveness, fosters a positive work environment, and sets a powerful example for others within the organization. By taking care of themselves, women in leadership can sustain their performance and impact over the long term, contributing to their organizations and communities in significant and lasting ways.

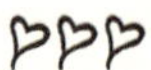

"Each step taken by a woman in leadership paves
the way for more voices to be heard and more
stories to be acknowledged."

♥♥♥

NINETEEN
Global Perspectives on Women in Power

The role of women in positions of power and leadership has become a focal point in global discussions on gender equality and empowerment. Across different cultures and political systems, women's ascent to power is reshaping policies, economies, and societies. Understanding the global landscape of women in leadership roles offers insight into the progress made and the challenges that persist in achieving gender parity in power.

Diversity in Leadership Across the World

Globally, the representation of women in leadership roles varies significantly by region, culture, and sector. In some countries, women have made substantial inroads into the highest levels of leadership, including heads of state and government positions. For instance, countries like New Zealand, Germany, and Finland have demonstrated strong female leadership at national levels. In contrast, in other regions, cultural norms and societal structures still significantly limit women's roles in leadership, often relegating them to less visible or influential positions.

Barriers to Women's Leadership Globally

Despite progress, several universal barriers hinder women's full participation in leadership:

Cultural Stereotypes: In many cultures, traditional gender roles still play a significant role in defining what is considered appropriate for women, often excluding them from leadership roles or the political arena.

Structural Barriers: These include discriminatory laws and practices that inhibit women's access to education, finance, and even the legal rights needed to ascend to positions of power.

Political and Economic Barriers: Women often face challenges in breaking into the political sphere or climbing corporate ladders due to lack of networks, mentorship, and the glass ceiling effect.

Violence and Discrimination: In some regions, active discrimination and violence aimed at preventing women from claiming or exercising power remain profound challenges.

Effective Strategies for Promoting Women in Leadership

Several strategies have been effectively employed across different regions to promote women in leadership:

Legislative Reforms: Quotas and affirmative action policies have been used in places like Rwanda, India, and several Scandinavian countries to ensure women's representation in political or leadership roles.

Education and Empowerment Programs: Global initiatives aim to empower women through education, leadership training, and capacity building, which are crucial for preparing women to assume leadership roles.

Economic Incentives: Programs that provide economic incentives for businesses to promote women, or for women to start their own businesses, help in creating more opportunities for women to lead.

Public Awareness Campaigns: These campaigns promote gender equality and the importance of women's leadership in societal development, helping to shift public perceptions and cultural norms.

Impact of Women in Leadership Roles

The impact of women in leadership roles can be observed in various areas:

Policy Changes: Women leaders often advocate for policies that support social welfare, education, and health, benefiting society at large. Studies have shown that countries with more women in government tend to have more comprehensive welfare policies.

Economic Growth: Diverse leadership teams, including those with women, are often more innovative and effective, leading to better economic outcomes.

Societal Benefits: Leadership by women contributes to more equitable societies. It challenges existing stereotypes and inspires future generations of women to seek leadership roles.

Challenges in Women's Leadership

Women in power often face unique challenges:

Higher Standards: Women leaders are often held to higher standards than their male counterparts and may face greater scrutiny.

Isolation: Being among the few or the only woman in a leadership position can lead to isolation and lack of support.

Work-Life Balance: Managing the demands of leadership roles and personal or family responsibilities can be particularly challenging for women.

The global perspective on women in power illustrates both significant progress and considerable challenges. While the path to gender parity in leadership is complex and fraught with barriers, the continued advocacy for and investment in women's leadership globally is crucial. The success stories and the positive impacts observed where women have attained and exercised power provide compelling arguments for more inclusive and equitable leadership structures worldwide. As societies continue to evolve, the role of women in leadership will undoubtedly be a critical factor in shaping the future, promoting sustainable development, and achieving greater social justice.

ᗫᗫᗫ

"Global perspectives on women in power illustrate not just the challenges faced but the shared ambition and hope for a more inclusive world."

❤❤❤

TWENTY

THE FUTURE OF WOMEN'S LEADERSHIP: TRENDS AND PREDICTIONS

The trajectory of women's leadership is a topic of significant importance and interest as societies globally move towards more inclusive and equitable frameworks. Observing current trends and anticipating future developments is crucial for understanding how women will shape and transform leadership roles across various sectors in the coming years. This analysis helps in preparing for changes and ensuring that the progress in gender equality continues.

Emerging Trends in Women's Leadership

Several key trends are currently shaping the landscape of women's leadership:

Increased Representation in Politics and Business

Globally, there is a gradual but steady increase in the number of women holding significant positions in politics and business. This trend is expected to continue as more women gain access to education and professional opportunities, and as societal attitudes towards women in leadership roles evolve. Initiatives and policies promoting gender diversity, such as gender quotas and affirmative action, are likely to further bolster this trend.

Greater Focus on Diversity and Inclusion

Organizations are increasingly recognizing the value of diversity and inclusion in driving innovation, reflecting customer markets, and enhancing decision-making processes. This recognition is pushing more companies and institutions to implement policies that actively promote the inclusion of women in leadership positions. The future will likely see diversity and inclusion becoming standard practice, rather than a special initiative.

Technological Advancements and the Digital Economy

The rise of the digital economy is opening new avenues for women to lead, particularly in sectors that have traditionally been male-dominated. Technology not only facilitates flexible working arrangements that can help women balance work and personal life but also provides platforms for women to start and grow their own businesses with relatively low overhead costs.

Leadership in Sustainability and Social Responsibility

Women are increasingly seen as leaders in sustainability and social responsibility movements. Their leadership in these areas is often associated with a more collaborative and inclusive approach, which is critical in addressing complex global challenges such as climate change, inequality, and social justice.

Predictions for the Future of Women's Leadership

Based on current trends, several predictions can be made about the future of women's leadership:

Normalization of Women in Top Leadership Roles

As more women enter and succeed in leadership roles, it will become increasingly normal and expected to see women leading major corporations, governments, and other influential organizations. This normalization will help in breaking down the remaining psychological and institutional barriers that currently hinder women's leadership ascent.

Leadership Styles Will Evolve

The leadership style typically associated with women, which often emphasizes empathy, inclusiveness, and collaboration, will likely become more mainstream as the efficacy of this style in modern governance and business is continuously validated. This shift may also influence how leadership is taught in academic and professional settings.

Enhanced Support Structures

It is anticipated that there will be an increase in structures and networks designed to support women in leadership roles. This includes mentorship programs, professional networks, and family-friendly workplace policies that make it easier for women to pursue and sustain leadership positions.

Impact on Global Challenges

Women leaders will play crucial roles in addressing global challenges, bringing new perspectives and solutions to issues such as poverty, education, health care, and climate change. Their involvement in these areas will be critical in crafting effective and sustainable strategies.

Continued Need for Advocacy and Change

Despite progress, ongoing advocacy for gender equality in leadership will remain essential. Structural inequalities, unconscious bias, and cultural resistance to women in power are likely to persist as issues requiring continued effort and attention.

The future of women's leadership looks promising but requires persistent efforts to overcome existing challenges. The trends and predictions indicate a world in which leadership is more reflective of the gender diversity of the population, leading to richer, more effective, and just governance and management in all sectors of society. The continued rise of women in leadership roles will not only transform traditional leadership paradigms but will also play a crucial role in addressing some of the most pressing issues facing the world today.

"Leading with grace means leveraging one's
inherent strengths, fostering unity, and leading by
example, qualities that many women naturally
bring to leadership roles."

💗💗💗

Citation And References

This book represents the culmination of extensive research and meticulous analysis, incorporating a diverse range of sources, including numerous books, scholarly studies, and personal experiences. Additionally, I have scoured various websites to gather relevant information and data essential for the compilation of this work. I have taken every precaution to ensure the accuracy of the information presented and have diligently cited all sources to acknowledge their contributions.

Despite these efforts, the possibility of inadvertent errors remains. I deeply value the insights of my readers and appreciate any feedback that can help identify and rectify such inaccuracies. I encourage you to bring any discrepancies to my attention.

Your feedback is not only welcome but crucial, as it will aid in correcting current editions and enhancing the content of future ones. I am committed to maintaining the highest standards of accuracy and reliability in my work and thank you for your support and understanding.

Additionally, I firmly uphold the principle of freedom of speech and expression as guaranteed under Article 19(1)(a) of the Constitution of India, and I respect the diverse viewpoints and expressions of all readers.

ϷϷϷ

Other Books Of The Author

1. Empowering Minds: A Journey into Women's Self-Discovery and Power
2. The Dynamics of Motivation: Catalyzing Thought into Action
3. Meditation and Mental Well Being: The Path to Inner Peace and Clarity
4. The Psychology of Child Education: Nurturing Future Generations
5. Ethical Enlightenment: A Modern Guide to Living with Integrity
6. Voices of Empowerment: Stories of Women Rising Against Odds
7. Social Psychology in Everyday Life: Understanding Human Connections
8. The Essence of Motivational Speaking: Inspiring Change in Others
9. Balancing Acts: Women, Work, and the Will to Lead
10. Guiding with Grace: Raising Children with Compassion and Awareness
11. The Power of Positive Aging: Embracing Life After Fifty
12. Building Resilient Communities: Social Work in Action
13. The Ethical Educator: Principles for Teaching and Learning
14. From Insight to Impact: Social Psychology for a Better World
15. The Ethics of Empathy: A Guide to Ethical Living
16. The Science of Empowering the Self: Navigating Life's Challenges with Psychological Wisdom
17. The Mindful Conscious Leader: Meditation Techniques for Modern Management
18. Pioneering Spirit: Women's Pathways to Leadership and Empowerment
19. Feeling to Healing: The Role of Emotional Intelligence in Child Development
20. Transformative Talks and Words of Inspiration: Insights into Motivational Oratory

❧❧❧

Contact

Dr. Minakshi Bansal
Social Activist
Ahmedabad, Gujarat, Bharat
minakshiindiag20@yahoo.com

❦❦❦

|| LOKAHA SAMASTHAHA SUKHINO BHAVANTU ||

• 133 •